MW01504522

Mi
CARA

Letters from heaven –
FOR SUCH A TIME AS THIS

Esther 4:14

W. A. VEGA

PRESS

To You ~ Today

Mi CARA

Letters from heaven -
FOR SUCH A TIME AS THIS...

Esther 4:14

W. A. VEGA

Mi
CARA

Letters from heaven –
FOR SUCH A TIME AS THIS...

Esther 4:14

Mi Cara

Introduction

Can we talk? Really talk, openly, sincerely, about what matters most: life. Our life—today.

It was during a very, very challenging season of my life when I was awakened to the words "Mi Cara" as if whispered in my inner ear. The voice was soft and tender. Perhaps it was my imagination, but I could almost feel warm air on my face as these words were whispered. I turned to my husband, but all I heard was the rhythmic sound of his breathing.

He was soundly asleep. It was not him, so I surmised that this was just my imagination, turned and went back to sleep.

I heard the same words and the voice again, spoken softly and tenderly. This time, I knew it was the voice of my Beloved Lord who had whispered into my spirit. Even though I did not know what the words meant when it was spoken, I knew it was personal and intimate, and filled with affection. I can't recall how I responded, but according to my journal entry the next day, I snuggled even closer to my husband and continued sleeping. How unspiritual!

The next day, I learned the meaning of the words I heard the previous night. My husband who was bilingual (Spanish/English), told me that "cara" means "face" in Spanish, and "mi" means "my." The Lord had whispered, "My face … my face." Even though I did not realize the impact of those tender words at the time, it became an anchor in the tsunami to come.

I also learned that the words reversed "Cara Mia," means "My Beloved." My sister, my friend, I hear the Lord whispering these same words to us today. To you and me — now — in our present circumstances.

He is calling out to us as His Beloved, as His Face, in this season, in this generation "For such a time as this" (Esther 4:14).

Mi Cara, these letters from heaven are for you. It's for you and me to better understand the heart of our beloved Lord and Father as He desires to speak to us in our current season from His Word.

I began writing these letters in 2000. I was inspired by God's Word as I listened to many women share their stories. I imagined what our Heavenly Father and Lord would say to His daughters in various seasons and experiences of our lives based on His written word, the Bible. I have shared these letters from heaven with many ladies over time as the Holy Spirit would lead and I'm always amazed at how the Lord would direct just the right letter to the right woman to speak to her in her current season. It's the same for you today.

These letters from heaven are not intended to be read in sequence, as there is no logical sequence to where it is placed in the pages. Might I suggest that you allow the Holy Spirit to direct you to the letter He wants you to read today?

As women, we share a common bond of experiences. I invite you to journey with me through the experiences we choose, and the experiences which choose us, (welcomed and unwelcomed).

The purpose of these letters is to allow us to:

- Better understand the Father heart of God to His daughters in various seasons of life;
- Hear His voice speaking to us, personally and intimately through His written word, for such a time as this;
- Grow more deeply in a personal and intimate relationship with our Heavenly Father;
- Better understand and empathize with each other as we share a common bond of experiences; and
- *Love* more deeply as we are loved by our Lord.

Then we can *encourage* each other on our adventure through life on earth, *embrace* the whole truth of the Gospel of Jesus Christ and see how relevant it is for us today and *emerge* gloriously as eagles, soaring in high places through every experience and season of life.

Dedication

*T*his book is dedicated to my daughter, Carlan, without whom I would not have the unspeakable joy of my three precious and beautiful granddaughters, Myah, Makayla and Emma, and all the women who have influenced my life. To every mother, daughter, granddaughter, grandmother, sister, niece, aunt, god-mother, god-daughter, step-daughter, friend: *thank you for being there.*

My heart is also very grateful to my Lord for allowing me to see just a tiny glimpse of His tender heart of love, compassion, and understanding to His dear daughters. We are His daughters if we have accepted His invitation to receive His Son, Jesus Christ into our lives as Savior and Lord.

Mi Cara, His Beloved, His Face—He calls you "Highly Favored," for you are His favorite and He loves you just as you are today!

I also want to thank every woman who has shared their stories with me over the years. I listened. More importantly, God listened and He has a plan for your life.

"For such a time as this..." Esther 4:14

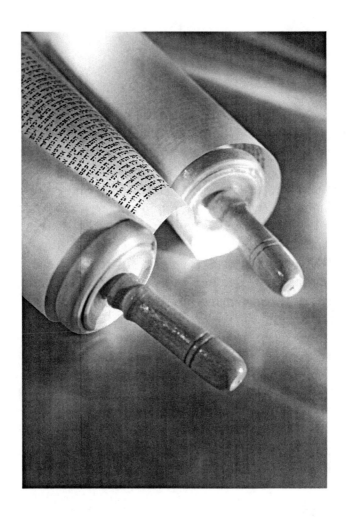

Letter 1

"I am dark, but lovely,

O daughters of Jerusalem,

Like the tents of Kedar

Like the curtains of Solomon.

Do not look upon me, because I am dark,

Because the sun has tanned me

Like a lily among thorns,

So is my love among the daughters."

Song of Solomon 1

How beautiful are your feet in sandals,

O prince's daughter!

The curves of your thighs are like jewels,

The work of the hands of a skillful workman."

Song of Solomon 7:1

Today

Mi Cara,

You are my great delight, my absolute joy and my precious, precious prize. I conceived you when I created the foundation of this world and, even before I brought you into existence, I cherished you.

As an expectant father, my thoughts were always of you and I longed for the day when you acknowledged me as your Father. I was there when you were conceived in the secret place. I saw your body being knitted together, and I fashioned you with my own hands.

You are my special artwork, created in my own image. You see, my daughter, as a father, I get an indescribable joy seeing my children look just like me.

I know there are times, Daughter, when you gaze in the mirror and you don't see the beauty I created. I hear your disappointment, wishing that I had created you differently. My heart aches when I see your disappointment, for I long for you to see the beauty I see.

Your beauty is not in your outward appearance, which will one day fade away. Your beauty is in the kindness of your speech, the gentleness of your touch, the compassion of your tears and, most of all, the availability and readiness of your heart to be delighted in me.

My beautiful one, gaze in the mirror again, and allow me to transform your vision so that you, too, can see the beauty I see.

Your Father

Ephesians 1; Psalm 139; Ephesians 5; Proverbs 31

Your response: Date_____

Dear Father,

_____

_____

_____

_____

_____

_____

_____

_____

_____

_____

_____

_____

_____

_____

_____

_____

_____

_____

_____

Your daughter,

Letter 2

"I do not count myself to have apprehended;

but one thing I do,

forgetting those things which are behind

and reaching forward to those things which are ahead,

I press toward the goal for the prize of the

upward call of God in Christ Jesus.

Therefore let us, as many as are mature,

have this mind; and if in anything you think

otherwise, God will reveal even this to you.

Nevertheless, to the degree that we have already attained,

let us walk by the same rule, let us be of the same mind..."

Philippians 3:13–16

Today

My Precious Daughter,

How I long to be known by you! You already know Me as God, but I want you to know Me as your friend, as the One who loves you most, as your Everlasting Father, your Redeemer and your Prince of Peace.

I understand why you have kept Me at a distance and I understand your hurt and suspicion of anyone who wants to draw close to you. I know the horror of your past and the depth of your pain. I understand how difficult it is to forgive those who have hurt you so deeply. I weep with you over that hurt. My child, I really do understand. I also understand why you hold Me, your Heavenly Father, responsible and why you question My love for you.

Draw closer child so that you can see why I understand so fully. Look into the ragged edges where they rammed a spear through my Son's side, and stare at the deep puncture wounds in His hands. Gaze at the deep gash in His head from the crown of thorns and the holes in His feet from where they pound the nails. Draw closer and see His back, barely visible for the blood, look closer still and see My tears as blood rolled down His face and hear Him whisper "forgive them for they know not what they do." Luke 23:34

Come even closer and feel His shame as the ones I love publically paraded His naked body and spat on it as if He were worse than a murderer. He listened to their false accusations, their jeering, and lewd shouts and saw the hatred in their eyes, but the worst pain of all was His feeling of being abandoned and forsaken by Me, for I have never been apart from My Son.

My precious, precious child, I allowed this horror to My Son, My only Son, for you. My Son, "for the joy that was set before Him, endured the cross, despising the shame, and has sat down at the right hand of the throne of God." Heb 12:1–3

My daughter, you are Our joy. Sin separated you from relationship with Me, your Heavenly Father, and as a Father, I was heartbroken by this separation, so I made a way and sent My Son, My only Son, to take on the penalty of sin. "For He made Him who knew no sin to be sin for us, that we might become the righteousness of God in Him." 2 Cor 5:21

My daughter, My Son, My only Son, Jesus Christ has paid the price for sin, past, present and future. "For as the heavens are high above the earth, so great is His mercy toward those who fear Him; as far as the east is from the west, so far has He removed our transgressions from us. As a father pities his children, so the Lord pities those who fear (love) Him. For He knows our frame; He remembers that we are dust." Psalm 103:11–14

Little one, because you are completely forgiven, now you must forgive. I desire that you come closer... even closer but your unforgiving heart will keep us apart. I know it's difficult to forgive, but I will correct every wrong and punish every evil. If you understand the horror and consequences of sin as I do, you would ask for My mercy upon all those who have hurt you.

Remember that I "shall not be mocked, whatsoever man sows, that shall he also reap." Gal 6:7

My precious little one, come nearer that I may heal all your hurts. Give Me every hurt, and every hardship you have endured and I shall give you My joy, My love, My Holy Spirit to live within you, to enable you to be all that I have designed and desire for you to be before the foundation of the world.

Come closer and let's grow deeper in our relationship.

Abba Father

Isaiah 9; PS 147; John 10; Matt 6; Rom 6

Your response: Date_____
Dear Father,

_____

_____

_____

_____

_____

_____

_____

_____

_____

_____

_____

_____

_____

_____

_____

_____

_____

_____

_____

Your Daughter,

Letter 3

"Come unto me
   all those who are weary
   and heavy laden
   and I will give you rest…
   Take my yoke
   upon you
   for it is easy and light."
   Matt 11:28

Today

Dearest Daughter,

You are a wonderful companion and friend. My heart skips with delight when you awake and your first thoughts are of Me. If you only know how I anticipate when you come to Me, regardless of the amount of time you spend, or the reasons for your coming. I simply enjoy when we are together.

There have been many times when I wanted to meet your needs, to quiet your troubled heart, or to give you peace beyond your understanding, but you didn't ask. I've watched you go to other people, and I've seen you go to familiar places and activities that give you momentary satisfaction. I've watched you avoid Me when I was ready and willing to answer your need.

There have even been times when you asked and invited My wisdom and will, but you immediately go about meeting those needs yourself. My heart is crushed during those times because you don't really believe that I love you enough to take care of you and meet your simplest needs.

I enjoy being asked and will never become weary or frustrated by your coming to Me. I hear your need the first time. In fact, child, I know your needs before you even ask, but you must ask, and then you must trust. It's not bothersome if you continue asking until you have what you need. You see child, when you continually come to Me to ask, even if it's for the same needs, you are spending time with Me and acknowledging Me as your Father. I love the time you spend with Me!

As your All Knowing Father, I want you to trust Me unconditionally. My timing is perfect, although it is different from yours, I am never late. As you trust Me and wait upon Me, you will begin to understand more and more how I go about meeting your needs.

Child, don't become confused by false teachers who give you magical formulas of how to get what you want from Me. My ways are so different and My thoughts so greater than any man's. I cannot be manipulated. I am God. I am your Father and I deal with each child personally and intimately.

What I desire is that
you talk with Me,
ask of Me,
trust in Me and
wait for Me.

I guarantee you will not be disappointed, nor will you ever be ashamed.

Your adoring Father

John 15; James 4; Psalm 27; Psalm 62; Isaiah 40

Your response: Date_____

Dear Father,

_____

_____

_____

_____

_____

_____

_____

_____

_____

_____

_____

_____

_____

_____

_____

_____

_____

_____

Your daughter,

Letter 4

"But Zion said, "The Lord has forsaken me, and my Lord has forgotten me."

"Can a woman forget her nursing child?

And not have compassion on the son of her womb?

Surely they may forget.

Yet I will not forget you.

See, I have inscribed you on the palms of My hands;

Your walls are continually before Me..."

Isaiah 49:15–16

Today

My precious daughter,

How could I ever forget you when you have been with Me since the foundation of the world? You are forever part of Me. I sealed our relationship when I allowed My Son to die on the cross. Now you are in me, because He is in you. My Spirit dwells in you and I am with you always.

My daughter, let me shout on the rooftop of your heart that I will never, ever, no, not ever, leave you, forsake you or deny you, no matter what. I will *never* abandon you or reject you because you are a vital part of me. I have sworn this by myself, and there is none greater to swear by, that I am committed to be with you always.

Daughter, believe my tears as they roll down my face and as my heart explodes in pieces, as I rejected my own Son, my only Son, all to secure relationship with you forever. Child, if I am willing to do this, please know that there is nothing, absolutely nothing that could ever separate you from My love.

There is *nothing* that you could do to prevent My total and complete love for you. Little one, above all, I want you to feel the security of My love and presence in your life, now and forever. Just look to the cross.

Forever in love with you....
Abba

John 15; Heb 14; Matt 28; Rom 8

Your response: Date_____

Dear Father,

_____

_____

_____

_____

_____

_____

_____

_____

_____

_____

_____

_____

_____

_____

_____

_____

_____

_____

Your daughter,

Letter 5

"Now may the God of peace Himself sanctify you completely and may your whole spirit, soul, and body be preserved blameless at the coming of our Lord Jesus Christ.

He who calls you is faithful, who also will do it."

1 Thessalonians 5:23–24

Today

Dear Daughter,

You hold a very special and unique position in my family because I chose you and adopted you. Yes, child, even knowing everything about you, including the number of hair on your head, I chose you and call you my own. Not only have I chosen you, and call you "daughter," but I have given you my name and have joined myself to you by the blood of my Son, Jesus.

You are a vital part of my family and only you can fill that position. Don't be intimated little one, because I will not give you a position that you cannot fill. I will also equip you with everything you need. My Spirit will be with you always.

Remember when Jesus first called His disciples, He said, "follow Me, and I will make you." I am still committed to making you to become what I have destined you to be and I have never failed, nor will I ever give up.

I have already begun the molding process, which I know you find uncomfortable. It is difficult to understand now, daughter, but the very discomfort you are experiencing is what will make you strong and equip you to fill the position I have for you.

I desire above all that during this process, you will not lean on your own understanding, because that only causes confusion, doubt and more discomfort. Instead, trust Me as your loving Father to know what and who I am making you to be. When you cannot trust My hand, trust My heart child which is always full of love for you.

Love you…
Abba

Eph 1; Gal 3; Eph 2; Eph 4; Proverbs 3

Your response: Date_____

Dear Father,

_____

_____

_____

_____

_____

_____

_____

_____

_____

_____

_____

_____

_____

_____

_____

_____

_____

_____

_____

Your daughter,

Letter 6

"Many women have done excellently,
but you surpass them all.
Charm is deceitful, and beauty is
vain, but a woman who fears the
LORD is to be praised. Give her of
the fruit of her hands, and let her
works praise her in the gates."

Proverbs 31: 30–31

Today,

My Beloved,

You are a mother after my own heart! I have seen you nurture your children and train them up in the way that they should go. You have taught them values and principles according to My Word. You have invested time and resources into their development. Most importantly, I have seen you on your knees crying out for them and have heard every prayer.

Despite your care, nurturing, teaching and example, they have chosen their own path and their own way. I have seen your disappointment and pain as you watch them make poor choices. Choices that are destructive to themselves and others; and I have watched you blame yourself for every wrong choice.

Daughter, I understand. I understand the heartache and pain of watching your own children make poor choices. I began with two children and raised them in a perfect place and taught them My ways. I poured all My love, attention and affection into them and desired that they would be like Me.

Instead, they chose a different path—a path that led to sin and death. I did not give up, and I will never give up. Let me encourage you from My own experience and example, to never give up.

I continue to pursue My children in love, mercy, grace and compassion. I will never give up My passionate pursuit for my children. I have even provided a path for them to return to My loving arms, and I stand and watch, waiting and longing to see them return to Me.

Oh daughter, your pain and disappointment is real and it's temporary. It's the same pain that I experienced with My children's wrong choice in a garden some time ago, and it's the same pain I feel today when I see My children choose their own path. I have good news, daughter. My word is true and shall not return to Me void. Though you see no change today, as you take one day at a time to

Wait
Watch
Pray

You will see your children return to the values and principles that you taught them. Don't ever give up. I am with you and I am with them.

Love,
Your Father

Prov 22; Luke 15; Gen 3; Matt 18; Isaiah 55

Your response: Date_____

Dear Father,

_____

_____

_____

_____

_____

_____

_____

_____

_____

_____

_____

_____

_____

_____

_____

_____

_____

_____

_____

Your daughter,

Letter 7

"Who shall separate us from the love of Christ?

Shall tribulation, or distress, or persecution, or famine, or nakedness, or danger, or sword?

As it is written, "For your sake we are being killed all the day long;

we are regarded as sheep to be slaughtered."

No, in all these things we are more than conquerors through him who loved us.

For I am sure the neither death nor life, nor angels nor rulers, nor things present nor things to come, nor powers, nor height nor depth, nor anything else in all creation will be able to separate us from the love of God in Christ Jesus our Lord."

Rom 8:35–39

Today

Daughter,

You are such a champion! And with My Spirit living within you, you will succeed. Remember that you can do all things through My Son, Jesus Christ, for you are more than a conqueror through Him! And all things will work together for your good because you love Me and are called according to My purposes for your life.

My courageous child, I am confident that you will finish the race that I have set before you and you will receive the prize of My upward call for your life. Let me gently remind you that as a champion running this race of life, you should not get entangled with the things of this world, which is fleeting and perishing.

Keep your eye little one on the finish line, and as a long distance runner, pace yourself to finish the course.

I have designed you to be a vessel of gold and precious metal, ready and available for My work. So stay focused on the course I have set before you, keeping your eye on My Son, Jesus Christ, who is the author and finisher of your faith.

All my Love,
Your Abba, Father

Jos 1; Rom 8; 2 Tim 4; 1 Cor 9; Heb 12;
Gal 5; 2 Tim 2

Your response: Date_____

Dear Father,

_____

_____

_____

_____

_____

_____

_____

_____

_____

_____

_____

_____

_____

_____

_____

_____

_____

_____

Your daughter,

Letter 8

"But without faith it is impossible

to please Him,

for he who comes to God

must believe that He is,

and that He is a rewarder

of those who diligently seek Him..."

Hebrews 11:6

Today

My Dearest Daughter,

You are my delicate flower, a sweet fragrance to Me. I've watched over you all your life and know the depth of your endurance. You allowed Me to carry you when the pain of disappointment, rejection and persecution would have overwhelmed you.

You embraced hope even when most would have given up. Even through your tears, you allowed My goodness to show. I've watched you grow, delicate one, through storms and droughts and know that your roots are deep and strong.

I am pleased with you and have reserved a special place in my presence for great is your reward because you have been faithful.

Forever,
Your Adoring Father

Phil 4; PS 1; Rev 22

Your response: Date_____

Dear Father,

_____

_____

_____

_____

_____

_____

_____

_____

_____

_____

_____

_____

_____

_____

_____

_____

_____

Your daughter,

Letter 9

".... For the Lord God is a sun and shield;

The Lord will give grace and glory:

No good thing will He withhold

From those who walk uprightly.

O Lord of hosts,

Blessed is the man who trusts in You!"

Psalm 84:11–12

Today

My Dear Daughter,

When I look at you, I see a pure, innocent, sinless, lovely child, whom I love dearly and accept completely. There is nothing you can do to make Me love or accept you more than I already do, so please stop trying.

My Son sealed your acceptance on the Cross. "It is finished." John 19:30. It truly is finished, so please stop trying to earn My acceptance and love.

I know it may be difficult to understand, but as your Father, I want to be your provider of everything. I want to and I am delighted to meet your every need. More than anything, I want you to totally and completely depend on My unlimited resources. No good thing will I withhold from you because you love Me.

My independent one, I want to transform you to a dependent one, and unlike what you may think, depending on Me takes strength and courage as I call you to walk by faith in My total love for you and not in what you can see or acquire for yourself.

I know that you have been striving to please Me by all the good things you do, but know that pleasing Me is simpler than you think.

All I desire is that you trust Me. For without faith it is impossible to please Me.

Your trustworthy Father,

Phil 4; PS 84; Matt 11; Heb 11; 2 Cor 5

Your response: Date_____

Dear Father,

_____

_____

_____

_____

_____

_____

_____

_____

_____

_____

_____

_____

_____

_____

_____

_____

_____

Your daughter,

Letter 10

"And we know

that all things

work together for good

to those who love God,

and to those who are called according to His
purpose…"

Romans 8:28

Today

My Lovely One,

I have heard your groaning and have seen your many tears. You are not alone; you are not forsaken. Your prayers are continually before Me and I have saved every tear. You have asked so many questions and I am the answer to all of them. I will not confuse you but if you allow Me, I will give you clarity of mind and show you things that only through My eyes you can see.

I understand that it is difficult to lift your head and look to Me. I hear your heart and want so much to let you know that I am working all things out for your good. If only I could mandate that you trust me. Daughter, I want your trust to be given willingly and freely. I will not violate your will. Because I love you so much, I am willing to wait.

How many times I longed to comfort you but you refused to be comforted by Me? How I long to show you great and miraculous things to hope for, but you refused to believe.

My child, I will not stop pursuing your affection. I will not stop extending My arms, nor will I withhold the good things I have for you. You are My child, you are My daughter, and I love you and want the best for you.

Look to me…

Your patiently waiting, Father

2Kings 20; 1 Cor 14; 1 Cor 2; PS 121; PS 84

Your response: Date_____

Dear Father,

_____

_____

_____

_____

_____

_____

_____

_____

_____

_____

_____

_____

_____

_____

_____

_____

_____

_____

Your daughter,

Letter 11

"He that dwells in the secret place

of the Most High

shall abide under the shadow of the Almighty."

Psalm 91

Today

Dearest Daughter,

Your enthusiasm and zeal for life is inspiring! I am delighted by your great excitement and readiness to do great things. You will accomplish great things for I know the plans I have for you, plans to prosper you and not to harm you, plans to give you a hope and a future.

My vivacious gazelle, as much as I enjoy watching you work for Me, I long to have you simply sitting at My feet. When you are still and quiet in My presence, I can fill you to an overflowing of My love, My grace, My mercy, My wisdom, My understanding, My peace, My kindness and My joy. Because daughter, I am so much more concerned with who you are, than what you do. I want you to be so filled to an overflowing with Me that it's from the overflow that you can give.

Come and sit a while with Me my child....

Your Loving Father

Phil 45; Eph 3; Jer 29

PS
My arms are strong enough to carry you!

Your response: Date_____

Dear Father,

_____

_____

_____

_____

_____

_____

_____

_____

_____

_____

_____

_____

_____

_____

_____

_____

_____

_____

_____

Your daughter,

Letter 12

" The Spirit of the Sovereign Lord is on me, because the LORD has anointed me to proclaim good news to the poor.

He has sent me to bind up the brokenhearted,

to proclaim freedom for the captives and release from darkness for the prisoners,

to proclaim the year of the LORD's favor and the day of vengeance of our God,

to comfort all who mourn, and provide for those who grieve in Zion-

to bestow on them a crown of beauty instead of ashes,

the oil of joy instead of mourning,

a garment of praise instead of a spirit of despair.

They will be called oaks of righteousness,

a planting of the LORD for the display of his splendor."

Isaiah 61 1–3

Today,

My beautiful princess,

I have watched you grow in beauty through trials, pain, disappointment, rejection, loneliness and betrayal. You are fair, My daughter, My love. Truly you have eyes of a dove that is always fixed on Me.

Out of your weakness and pain you encourage others. In your poverty you care for the poor. Springing from your broken heart, you smooth the crushed in spirit. Out of your darkness you offer light and hope to the destitute.

From your trials and bondage, you have grown in stately grace and elegance to reach those in captivity. Out of your grief and mourning, you have emerged victoriously. Beauty shall arise from your ashes and joy from your mourning.

Your inward beauty is growing more and more beautiful every day. Your quiet spirit illuminates like apples of gold on a setting of silver. Your words drip like honey. Surely great is your reward My daughter, My princess, My bride, My friend.

Almighty God, Abba

James 4; Song of Solomon 1; Isaiah 61; Prov 31; Prov 25; 1Peter 3; Matt 5; Luke 6

Your response: Date_____

Dear Father,

_____

_____

_____

_____

_____

_____

_____

_____

_____

_____

_____

_____

_____

_____

_____

_____

_____

Your daughter,

Letter 13

"Ask and it shall be given unto you,

seek and you shall find,

knock and the door will be opened unto you.

For those who seek, find and

those who knock,

the door shall be opened..."

Matt 7:7

Today

My Darling Daughter,

If a son asks his father for bread, will he give him a stone? How much more My precious daughter, will I provide for you if you ask? I am willing and ready to give, because it is My good pleasure to give bountifully to My children. Remember, there is nothing impossible for your Father and all good things come from above.

Let Me remind you little flower, that I am GOD, and I am your Father. I created the universe with a word. I spoke and the skies became, I breathe life and there is life, I keep the universe in perfect balance. There is nothing impossible for me. I know every fish in the sea and count the birds of the air with a glance. I have counted every cell in your being and know your every thought before it is. I am Almighty God, there is NONE greater, and I am your Father.

I measure the depth of the sky with My little finger, and hold the sun, the moon and the stars in its place. I designed every mountain and know every insect and every animal that ever was. With a word I command the wind and know each wave of the sea. I am above all. I know all and My greatest accomplishment is you.

Don't be intimidated by Me little one, for I am all that and more. Yet I simply want to be known as your Father. Let Me love you and show you the greatness I have planned for your life. You are and always will be my greatest design.

Your adoring Papa....

Matt 7; Jer 32; Job 12; Gen 2; Isaiah 63

Your response: Date_____

Dear Father,

_____

_____

_____

_____

_____

_____

_____

_____

_____

_____

_____

_____

_____

_____

_____

_____

_____

_____

_____

Your daughter,

Letter 14

"Sing, O barren woman,

you who never bore a child;

burst into song,

shout for joy,

you who were never in labor;

because more are the children of the desolate woman
than of her who has a husband"

says the LORD.

Isaiah 54:1

Today

My Beloved Daughter,

Please join Me in singing Hannah's song:

"My heart rejoices in the LORD; my strength is exalted in the LORD.

I smile at my enemies, because I rejoice in Your salvation.

No one is holy like the LORD, for there is none besides You,

Nor is there any rock like our God.

Talk no more so very proudly;

Let no arrogance come from your mouth,

For the LORD is the God of knowledge; And by Him actions are weighed.

The bows of the mighty men are broken,

And those who stumble are girded with strength.

Those who were full have hired themselves out for bread,

And the hungry have ceased to hunger.

Even the barren has born seven,

And she who has many children has become feeble.

The LORD kills and makes alive;

He brings down to the grave and brings up.

The LORD makes poor and makes rich;

He brings low and lifts up.

He raises the poor from the dust

And lifts the beggar from the ash heap,

To set them among princes

And make them inherit the throne of glory.

For the pillars of the earth are the LORD's,

And He has set the world upon them.

He will guard the feet of His saints,

But the wicked shall be silent in darkness.

For by strength no man shall prevail.

The adversaries of the LORD shall be broken in pieces;

From heaven He will thunder against them.

The Lord will judge the ends of the earth.

He will give strength to His king,

And exalt the horn of His anointed."

1 Sam 2:1–10

Your Father,

Your response: Date_____

Dear Father,

_____

_____

_____

_____

_____

_____

_____

_____

_____

_____

_____

_____

_____

_____

_____

_____

_____

_____

Your daughter,

Letter 15

"Those who wait upon the Lord

shall not be disappointed,

nor shall

they be ashamed."

Psalm 69:6

Today

My Delicate Flower,

    Your tears and prayers are a sweet fragrance to Me. I see your heart that desires to know Me, to be with Me, to please Me. I also see your heart that is heavy with loneliness, discouragement and disappointment.

    My daughter, trust Me to complete the work that I began in you, remember that I shall provide everything you need to accomplish My purposes. I see you My child. I always see you and can never forget you. The loneliness you are feeling now is because I am drawing you closer to Me. I am jealous over you Little One, but the time is coming when I will release you into My plan, which is for good and not for evil.

    I desire that you enter into my rest.... come Little One, rest, relax. I am God. I will do what I say.

I am in absolute control.

    There is nothing too difficult for Me. I can open any door and close any door, and I shall move heaven and earth to bring about My purposes in your life. You must trust Me and wait on My appointed time for change. You shall not be disappointment for waiting.

Your adoring Father,

2 Cor 2; Phil 1; Psalm 37; Matt 7; Luke 12;
Phil 4; 1 Sam 16; Gen 16; Gen 18; Jeremiah 32;
Luke 1; Rev 3; Isaiah 40; Psalm 27

Your response: Date_____

Dear Father,

_____

_____

_____

_____

_____

_____

_____

_____

_____

_____

_____

_____

_____

_____

_____

_____

_____

_____

Your daughter,

Letter 16

"Forgetting those things

that are behind,

I press forward

to the upward call of God,

through Christ Jesus."

Phil 3: 13

Today

My Cherished Child,

I chose you and adopted you to be My child. You did not choose Me. I first chose you and called you by name, and I still call you. I call you highly favored, precious and lovely.

Yes, daughter, I know your past. I also know your present and your future. I am God who sees the end from the beginning. I have cast your sins as far as the east is from the west and remember them no more, so please stop reminding me.

When I see you, I see a sinless child, clean and pure as if you never sinned, all because you accept the finished work of My Son, who took upon Himself the penalty of sin, so that My children can have life and that more abundantly.

You are a new creature My precious little one and I will qualify you to accomplish My will. In fact, it is My pleasure to do that which I have purposed in you and through you.

I love you little one and I'm so glad to have you in my family.

Daddy God

John 15; Eph 1; Isaiah 46; Ecc 3 & 7; PS 103;
2Cor 5; Rom 6; John 10

Your response: Date_____

Dear Father,

_____

_____

_____

_____

_____

_____

_____

_____

_____

_____

_____

_____

_____

_____

_____

_____

_____

_____

_____

Your daughter,

Letter 17

"Then I saw a new heaven and a new earth,

for the first heaven and the first earth had passed away,
and the sea was no more.

And I saw the holy city,

new Jerusalem, coming down out of heaven from
God prepared as a bride adorned for her husband.

And I heard a loud voice from the throne saying,

"Behold, the dwelling place of God is with man.

He will dwell with them, and they will be his people,
and God himself will be with them as their God.

He will wipe away every tear from their eyes,

and death shall be no more,

neither shall there be mourning,

nor crying,

nor pain anymore,

for the former things have passed away."

Rev 21:1–4

Today,

My daughter,

"Eyes have not seen, nor have ears heard, nor has it entered into the heart of man the things that God has prepared for those who love Him, to those who are called according to His purpose."

1 Cor 2:9

The best is yet to come.

"Taste and see that the Lord is good. Blessed is the one who trusts in Him!"

Abba,

PS 34:8

Your response: Date_____

Dear Father,

_____

_____

_____

_____

_____

_____

_____

_____

_____

_____

_____

_____

_____

_____

_____

_____

_____

_____

Your daughter,

Letter 18

"But seek first the kingdom of God

and His righteousness,

and all these things will be added to you."

Matt 6

Today

My Beautiful One,

Come away with me to a special place where we can be alone. Walk with me, and let us reason together. I wait each day to hear you call My name and My eyes lovingly search for you. You are truly My treasure, My song, My delight and My joy.

Come, drink from the fountain I have provided and your thirst will be quenched. I long to be your first love and fill every part of you with My tender, unfailing love. Come, in the busyness of your day, steal away with Me to a secret place where only we can share.

My hands are extended to you and my touch will always be gentle. Come, My sweet princess, My Bride, My chosen one, come and let Me smooth your aching soul with the security of my affection. Come and let Me refresh you with springs of living water. Come and let Me take all your burdens and sorrows and turn your mourning into dancing.

Come to Me My timid one, and I will give you beauty for ashes. Come to Me and I will clothe you with robes of royalty and place a crown of righteousness upon your head. Come to Me and let Me cover your sin and shame with the sacrifice of My Son. Let Me give you a new name, My name, where you were once called "forsaken," you will be called "chosen for royalty." Come my beloved, and walk with me.

Your Adoring Father

PS 91; Gen 3; Is 1; John 4; Song of Solomon 2; Is 61; Is 62; John 4; Rev 21

Your response: Date_____

Dear Father,

_____

_____

_____

_____

_____

_____

_____

_____

_____

_____

_____

_____

_____

_____

_____

_____

_____

_____

Your daughter,

Letter 19

"Draw close to God

and

He will draw close to you......"

James 4

Today

My Precious Daughter,

I miss the nearness of your heart and the tenderness of your song in praise, worship, thanksgiving and adoration. I see from afar your heart that was once open to Me beginning to close and I understand. You see child, I know that hope deferred makes the heart sick, but it is I who have deferred your hope because I desire to accomplish so much more in you than the realization of that hope.

Dear child, remember I see the end from the beginning, and I know you better than you know yourself. Your heart tells Me that you don't want to distance yourself from Me, but it's the only defense you know to protect yourself from fear, hurt, rejection and disappointment. Yet you are not comfortable with that distance and you don't understand why, but I do. It's because My Spirit lives within you. I am in you and you are in Me.

Regardless of how much distance you desire to put between us, you will always be drawn to Me because I am the One drawing you. Yet I understand your reluctance, your hesitation, and your fear. I am not angry or disappointed with you, but in order for Me to bring you to the place you hope for, you must walk this uneasy path.

You see child, I want you to trust Me as much in the dark as in the light. The things you hope for are from Me. I am the one who whispered them to your heart, and you shall not be disappointed.

I will make your hope a reality, in time and in My way. Remember how I gave life to your hope in times past? I have not changed. I will continue to bless you because I love you. You are My child and you will never be disappointed because you trusted in Me.

Bring your heart close again and let Me strengthen and comfort you, as I bring your hope to life.

Your Loving Father,

Prov 13; 1Cor 6; John 15; Heb 13; Rom 5

Your response: Date_____

Dear Father,

_____

_____

_____

_____

_____

_____

_____

_____

_____

_____

_____

_____

_____

_____

_____

_____

_____

_____

_____

Your daughter,

Letter 20

"He will wipe away every tear from their eyes,

and death shall be no more,

neither shall there be mourning,

nor crying, nor pain anymore,

for the former things have passed away."

Rev 21:4

Today

My Delicate One,

I see the waves upon waves of sorrow and grief that have invaded your life. You are not alone. I am with you. Though the storms may come, they shall not overtake you. Weeping may last for a night season, but joy comes in the morning.

Look to Me. Let Me carry you through this difficulty. I weep with you because I never planned for you to experience this pain, sorrow and grief. The road ahead will be challenging as you journey through the stages of grief and mourning. Even though the pain will seem unbearable, remember that in your darkest, blackest hour, the Son shall shine again in your life.

Read the inspired poem of the Footprints in the Sand again, and remember that I am carrying you through this season. I will hold you close and draw you near if you allow Me to, and together we shall walk through this difficulty into liberty, peace, perseverance, and maturity. You shall know that indeed I cause all things to work together for good, to those who love Me and who are called according to my purpose.

Remember Sarah, Naomi, Ruth, Tamar, Hannah and other women of faith who through sorrow, poverty, persecution and barrenness attained the promise their heart desired. Yet the promise they attained was temporary, for there is an everlasting promise that all those who trust and believe in my Son shall attain; the promise of everlasting light, joy, peace and life.

Oh child! I know it hurts so much now, but it will not hurt forever. I will heal you. I will bind up your wounds. I will provide for you. I will cause you to hear laughter again. I will cause you to see joy. I will cause you to celebrate life. I will bring about My purposes in your life. Draw close to Me during this time of deep pain as I draw close to you. Here are my arms Little One, Precious One... see Me as I run to you.

Your Papa,

Is 41, 43, 53, 58; PS 30; Deut 31; 1 Chron 28; Prov 1; 1 Cor 10; John 11; James 1, 1 Samuel 1; Jer 30

Your response: Date_____

Dear Father,

_____

_____

_____

_____

_____

_____

_____

_____

_____

_____

_____

_____

_____

_____

_____

_____

_____

_____

Your daughter,

Letter 21

"Be anxious for nothing;

but in everything by prayer

and supplication

with thanksgiving

let your requests be made known unto God."

Phil 4:6

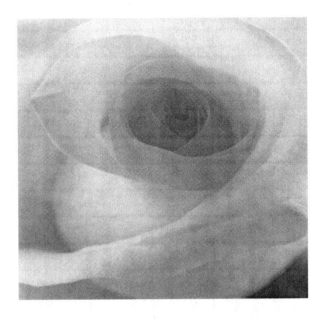

Today

My precious child,

I see your many anxieties. I hear your anxious thoughts as you lay awake at night. You are concerned about much, my little fish—concerned about things that you cannot control.

I also see the burdens you choose to carry, burdens that were never intended to be yours. You tell Me all the time how heavy they are, yet you refuse to lay them down and exchange them for My burdens, which are light and easy.

Delicate one, I hear you. I hear you asking for My help. I hear you repeating My promises and it excites Me that you're coming to Me and learning of Me from My written word. Yet I see you asking of Me one minute, and the next you are busy going about finding (and manipulating) possible solutions. My heart aches for you because I see you only getting more anxious and frustrated.

If you would only *relax, rest, wait* and allow Me to bring about My plan for you during this season. My precious one, I think you sometimes forget who I am. I am almighty God! And there is none other. There is nothing too difficult for Me.

My hand is not shortened that I can no longer save, nor are my ears deafened that I can no longer hear, and my eyes blinded that I can no longer see. I know the end from the beginning.

You have a choice my little one. You always have a choice. It's either My plan or yours. So choose carefully, my child, whom you will serve, either Me or your own will and desires.

Your Loving Heavenly Father,

Phil 4; 1Pet5; PS 31, 55, 68, 121, 138; Heb 4; 2Cor 4, 2Cor 1; Is 43, 59; Matt 7; Num 11; Joshua 24; Deut 30

Your response: Date_____

Dear Father,

_____

_____

_____

_____

_____

_____

_____

_____

_____

_____

_____

_____

_____

_____

_____

_____

_____

Your daughter,

Letter 22

"Casting all your care upon Him;

for he cares for you." 1 Pet 5

"When my father and my mother forsake me,

then the Lord will take me up…"

Psalm 27

Today

Dear Most Precious Jewel,

I created you for purpose, with purpose and on purpose. You are no accident. You are not a filthy rag to be tossed, bounced and trampled upon at whim. I conceived you in love and for love before the foundations of the world. Your worth far exceeds the rarest of jewels and your beauty surpasses the most perfect of sunsets. You are mine. You've always been My highly favored one.

Of all my creation, I treasure you most and will sacrifice My all just for you. Your worth is priceless. There is none like you in all my creation, uniquely designed, hand crafted, and perfectly formed and fashioned for My purposes. How I long for you to see your beauty through My eyes. Yet I see you gazing in the mirror and reflecting upon your own image, and the images strangers have painted of you.

Lift your head to Me—look to Me—You are beautiful and of much worth. Though the journey may be difficult, know and trust that I am with you and always will be with you to love you, to provide for you, to protect you—But you must trust Me enough to let go of your current circumstances.

Remember that I am God. I make rivers in the desert and streams in the wilderness. I will make a way where there is no way. I will open new paths for you.

Come with Me—Let Me lead you away from the distorted, perverted, and deceitful idea of love that explodes in anger and physical abuse. Let Me lead you to the love that I designed and desire for you.

Love that suffers long and is kind, love that does not envy; love that is not proud nor expresses itself rudely; love that does not seek its own; love that is not provoked; love that thinks no evil; love that bears all things, believes all things, hopes all things, and endures all things. Love that never fails.

This is the love I desire you to experience. Oh my child! My delicate one! My highly favored one! I weep when I see you beaten and tossed as a worthless rag. Will you trust Me? Will you trust My love for you?

Come away with me—You who are called "Forsaken" and "Worthless" and I will give you a new name, "Accepted" and "Precious."

Your Adoring Father,

PS 139; Song of Solomon 7; James 1;
Isaiah 43, 54 60 and 62; 1Cor 13

Your response: Date_____

Dear Father,

_____

_____

_____

_____

_____

_____

_____

_____

_____

_____

_____

_____

_____

_____

_____

_____

_____

_____

Your daughter,

Letter 23
Today

My precious flower,

"Greater love has no one than this that he lay down his life for his friends. You are My friends if you do whatever I command you. No longer do I call you servant, for a servant does not know what his master is doing; but I have called you friends."

John 15:13–15

I LOVE YOU.

Abba

Your response: Date_____

Dear Father,

_____

_____

_____

_____

_____

_____

_____

_____

_____

_____

_____

_____

_____

_____

_____

_____

_____

_____

Your daughter,

Letter 24

Shout for joy, O heavens; rejoice, O earth; burst into song. O mountains!

For the LORD comforts His people and will have compassion on His afflicted ones.

But Zion said, "The LORD has forsaken me, the Lord has forgotten me."

"Can a mother forget the baby at her breast and have no compassion on the child she has borne?

Thought she may forget,

I will not forget you!

See, I have engraved you on the palms of My hands;...."

Isaiah 49:13–16

Today

Dear Daughter,

Even a mother can forget the child of her womb but I will never forget you. You are mine. I am your God and I shall never, ever forget you.

I know the night seems long. You have been watching and waiting for Me to sovereignly change your season. You can trust that I will, in its appointed time. For I know the plans I have for you, plans to make you prosper, and not to harm you, and plans to give you hope and a future.

There are many things you don't understand now, but it will all come into perspective in its time. What you experience as disappointment today, you will see that it's opportunity tomorrow. What causes you to cry today, will bring you incredible joy tomorrow. What you're reluctant to let go of today will be multiplied tomorrow. What you see as delay today will be evidence of my providential plan for you in its perfect time.

My daughter, I will bring about the promises I've spoken into your heart by My Holy Spirit. I promise! Check My history, what I promise will surely come to pass. Not one of My words shall be returned unto Me void, but it shall accomplish the thing for which I send it forth.

So wait, just a little while longer, as I perfect My plans and My purposes for you, in My perfect timing and in My perfect way.

Yours Always,
Your Adoring Heavenly Father

Is 40, 49, 55, 58; Jer 29; Rom 8; 2Pet 1;
PS 27, 31, 105; Num 23; 1Cor 1; Deut 31; Luke 1

Your response: Date_____

Dear Father,

_____

_____

_____

_____

_____

_____

_____

_____

_____

_____

_____

_____

_____

_____

_____

_____

_____

Your daughter,

Letter 25

"Therefore the LORD waits to be gracious to you,

and therefore He exalts Himself to show mercy to you.

For the LORD is a God of justice;

Blessed are all those who wait for Him."

Isaiah 30

Today

My Adoring Daughter,

I remember our times together. Our early morning walks. Your songs of adoration during the night and your thoughts of Me throughout the day. I remember and I miss you. I miss your adoring looks, the flicker of your heart when you thought of my Son. The nearness and tenderness of your heart as you worship.

This love song was one of My favorites and I long to hear you sing it again to Me in our private, secret place:

Above all else, I want to know you, Lord
Above all else, I want to seek your face
Above all else, this world can offer me
Above my very life, itself
Above all else, You're above all else

Your life is very busy now. Filled with many worthwhile commitments to others, but not to Me. You say My name often, but your heart is far from Me and you know it. Come, stay a while with Me. Let us talk together. For though your heart is far from me, I desire to draw you near again.

Above all else, I desire you, your presence, your heart, your passion for My Son. Thank you for all the good things you do, and all the wonderful things you say of Me, but it's you I want. It's you I desire to spend time with. I desire to grow in friendship with you. Will you come away with me. I am drawing you now and will draw you again and again.

Your Loving Father,

Rev 2; Isaiah 29; James 4; Luke 4

Your response: Date_____

Dear Father,

_____

_____

_____

_____

_____

_____

_____

_____

_____

_____

_____

_____

_____

_____

_____

_____

_____

_____

Your daughter,

Letter 26

"But the Lord said to Samuel,

"Do not consider his appearance or

his height, for I have rejected him.

The Lord does not look at the things man looks at.

Man looks at the outward appearance,

but the LORD looks at the heart."

Samuel 16

Today

Dearest Daughter,

You have tremendous talent. You speak My name with passion and intensity. Your voice moves many to tears as you lead many in songs of worship. You know how to stir My people to emotional excitement, but I know that your heart is far from Me. You may fool many my child, but remember, you cannot fool Me.

I love you. You are my child and I shall never leave you nor forsake you. In fact, My daughter, I will leave the ninety nine and go after the one who is going astray.

That uncomfortable nudge you feel tugging at your heart, is Me. That knot you feel in your throat as you begin to sing or to speak in My Name, it's Me. That hesitation you feel on the inside, it's Me. I will continue to get your attention until you humble yourself under My hand, that I may exalt you in due season.

Listen—I will get your attention, for you are My child and I will not, I shall not, let you go. I know the praise and recognition you receive from others is intoxicating, but only for a brief moment. You already know that it does not nor can it ever compare to the joy, peace and acceptance you have when your heart is surrendered to Me.

Come, let us talk together. Though you have wandered away, I shall bring you near. I shall draw you near again with open arms for you are my child.

Your Loving Father,

Isaiah 29; Matt 15; Mark 7; Heb 13; Gal 1; John 5

Your response: Date_____

Dear Father,

_____

_____

_____

_____

_____

_____

_____

_____

_____

_____

_____

_____

_____

_____

_____

_____

_____

_____

Your daughter,

Letter 27

"Have I not commanded you?

Be strong and of good courage;

do not be afraid, nor be dismayed,

for the Lord your God is with you

wherever you go."

Joshua 1

Today

My dear Daughter,

I am teaching you how to stand alone with me. How to listen to me in the midst of a loud crowd. I am teaching you how to follow after me and it is a narrow road. Few find it, and narrow and difficult is the way.

But what I am teaching you today, in letting go of relationships, is a test. I will multiply back to you many relationships and those around you will be stunned at what I will accomplish in and through you.

Be strong and be courageous for it takes courage not to stand with the crowd. It takes courage to stand alone and to be a lone voice.... Look at my prophets, Jeremiah and Isaiah and so many others. Some were stoned, others killed, many mocked and laughed at because of their stance to speak what I tell them that was against popular teaching.

Be strong and courageous for you will need it in times to come. These small experiences are to strengthen you and to cause you to keep your eyes on Me no matter what.

My daughter, if you thought that in following me and surrendering to me that the world would applaud, you are wrong and I know you're disappointed. The world wants to follow after a god of their own image and making. They want to follow after a god they control. The message I have given you is not a popular one. Keep your eyes on Me and look to Me for validation. This will cost you everything, but remember that I am your exceedingly great reward.

Your Father, God

Psalm 91; Matt 7; Joshua 1; Jer 26

Your response: Date_____

Dear Father,

_____

_____

_____

_____

_____

_____

_____

_____

_____

_____

_____

_____

_____

_____

_____

_____

_____

_____

Your daughter,

Letter 28

"Therefore we do not lose heart.

Though outwardly we are wasting away,

yet inwardly we are being renewed day by day.

For our light and momentary troubles

are achieving for us an eternal glory

that far outweighs them all.

So we fix our eyes not on what is seen,

but on what is unseen.

For what is seen in temporary,

but what is unseen is eternal."

2 Cor 4: 16–18

Today,

Beautiful One—Mi Cara,

You are truly My face. My lovely face, crowned with honor and glory. I formed your innermost parts and watched you grow even while in your mother's womb. I formed and fashioned you inside and out. You are fearfully and wonderfully made. I designed you. You are My most beautiful and prized design in all My creation!

My beautiful one, with every passing day, month and year, I watch your real beauty sparkle and shine more and more. Oh! If you could see the beauty I see in every wrinkle, in every line, in every age spot, every pronounced vein and every grey hair!

You see, my daughter, I've watched you grow into the beauty you are today. I see you glow in every smile through pain. I see you shine brighter and brighter through every sorrow and grief this life offers. I see you grow stronger through every trial and test you endure. Even though your hands may grow weaker, I see your touch growing stronger and more confident. Daughter, I do not see as man sees, for I see you as you are, today, yesterday and forever—Beautiful. Yes, I call you Beautiful—I call you Extraordinary—I call you exquisite—I call you, My Child.

Daughter, the day will come when you will see the eternal beauty I see. Beauty that grows deeper and stronger from the inside out. Beauty that is visible only to those who see with My eyes. My little one, let Me remind you that you are eternal. Your years on earth are only the beginning years in eternity with Me. Fix your eyes on Me as you gaze in the mirror and let Me show you the beauty I always see.

Your adoring Father,

Psalm 139; Prov 31; 1Peter 1; 1John 2; 1Sam 16

Your response: Date_____

Dear Father,

_____

_____

_____

_____

_____

_____

_____

_____

_____

_____

_____

_____

_____

_____

_____

_____

_____

_____

_____

_____

Your daughter,

Letter 29

"As the heavens are higher than the earth,

so are my ways higher than your ways

and my thoughts than your thoughts."

Isaiah 55

Today

My Dearest Daughter,

I see your crushed heart through your courageous smile. What you are experiencing is very, very difficult. I know; I watched my Son die. I know the hurt and agony of watching someone you love in pain and dying.

Child, I also understand your anger. You wonder why I did not intervene as you prayed and others interceded. I heard every prayer. While I know you cannot understand why I did not answer your prayer in the way you desired, I want you to know that I did answer your prayer.

Your loved one is with Me, perfectly well, and rejoicing in what eyes have not seen, nor ears heard, of the things I have prepared for those who love Me. If you see him now, you too would rejoice.

But I know you're in tremendous pain and concerned about how you will live without him. I am here, and if you will invite Me, I will lead you through this tremendous pain to life, and that more abundantly.

Remember Naomi and Ruth, both destitute widows with no hope of redemption. Yet they chose to move forward into a new place and there stepped into the redemption I had planned for them. So I desire to lead you to a new place and a new season, but you must choose to take hold of My hand, even though you don't understand the path I am leading

you to. Like David and countless others you will join
in and say:

The Lord is my Shepherd; I shall not want.
He makes me to lie down in green pastures;
He leads me beside the still waters.
He restores my soul;
He leads me in the paths of righteousness
For His name same.
Yea, though I walk through the valley of the shadow
of death,
I will fear no evil;
For You are with me;
Your rod and Your staff, they comfort me.
You prepare a table before me in the presence of my
enemies;
You anoint my head with oil;
My cup runs over.
Surely goodness and mercy shall follow me
All the days of my life;
And I will dwell in the house of the Lord
Forever
Psalm 23
Will you choose My hand and let Me lead you?

Your Shepherd,
Abba

James 1; Job 28; PS 27; PS 91; PS 18; Ruth

Your response: Date_____

Dear Father,

_____

_____

_____

_____

_____

_____

_____

_____

_____

_____

_____

_____

_____

_____

_____

_____

_____

_____

Your daughter,

Letter 30

"He was despised and rejected by men,

a man of sorrows, and familiar with suffering.

Like one from whom men hide their faces he was despised,

and we esteemed him not."

Isaiah 53

Today

Dear Child,

I see your scars. The ones you hide on your wrists and on your heart. I know the extent of your pain and have longed for you to turn to Me for comfort. Oh, Little One, your life is precious, very precious to Me. I was there when you were conceived in your mother's womb and I numbered your days. I wept when I saw your attempts to shorten the days I have planned for you and longed for you to look to Me for comfort, purpose and value.

If you would only believe that the plan I have for you is for good and not for evil, to prosper you, to give you hope and a future. I am sad to see you despair of hope. Look to the Cross, where you will find true hope.

Oh delicate, precious flower, I see your pain and confusion. You have accepted many lies about your worth and value. This is from the evil one, the father of lies. I have seen your heart that yearns for truth, for acceptance, for love. Here I am. Look no further than the cross of My Son. Because of Him, you are fully accepted. You were purchased with a price beyond measure. Your life is precious, for I created you with purpose, for purpose and on purpose. You are no accident.

My priceless treasure, turn your heart to Me and let Me heal your hurt. Let Me ascribe to you value and worth and give you life, and that more abundantly.

Your Heavenly Father,

PS 139; PS 23; Jer 29; John 8

Your response: Date_____

Dear Father,

_____

_____

_____

_____

_____

_____

_____

_____

_____

_____

_____

_____

_____

_____

_____

_____

_____

_____

Your daughter,

Letter 31

"My soul magnifies the Lord,

And my spirit has rejoiced in God my Savior.

For He has regarded the lowly state of His maidservant;

For behold, henceforth all generations will call me blessed.

For He who is mighty has done great things for me

And holy is His name.

And His mercy is on those who fear Him

From generation to generation.

He has shown strength with His arm

He has scattered the proud in the imagination of their hearts.

He has put down the mighty from their thrones,

And exalted the lowly.

He has filled the hungry with good things,

And the rich He has sent away empty.

He has helped His servant Israel.

In remembrance of His mercy,

As He spoke to our fathers,

To Abraham and to his seed forever."

Luke 1

Today

Cara Mia,

How you delight My heart! As the deer pants for the water, so your heart pants after Me and it delights My heart. I love it when I see you wanting Me for Me, and not for what you hope I will give you. You truly delight My heart My child as I see My Son's reflection on your face.

My child, I trust you. I am so proud of you! I have heard your deep groaning in the night season through much weeping. I have seen you run to Me and fall in weakness and despair crying out for your enemies. I have seen you endure through pain, grief, disappointment, rejection, betrayal and loneliness. I feel the compassion of your heart for the widow, the orphan, the lost and hurting. Cara Mia, you are My courageous one, and I am proud of you.

I am proud with each choice you make that honors Me and puts Me first. I am proud of your stand for righteousness in the midst of a perverse culture. I am proud of your decision to follow hard after Me, obeying with joy and delight. I am proud that you held on to Me through the fire of life's challenges. Most importantly, I am so proud of how you adore My Son and your willingness to pick up your cross and follow after Him.

Oh Daughter, if you only knew how you delight My heart! And I will bless you beyond your greatest imagination. I will open windows and pour out blessings that you cannot contain. I will exalt you My child as you have humbled yourself in My hands, your enemies will see it and marvel.

Little one, I have plans for your future, plans to give you hope, plans to prosper the work of your hands, plans for good and not for evil.

I am God, and there is no other besides me who will move heaven and earth to bring my purposes to pass in your life.

Believe Me, child, even though today you see no sign of change, just as the leaves are turning brown and will fall to the ground, and the snow will come and cover the new life of spring, so shall your change come, and it will be glorious!

Your very proud Poppa

PS 37; Matt 6; PS 30; PS 27; PS 91; Deut 28; Jer 29; Habakkuk

Your response: Date_____

Dear Father,

_____

_____

_____

_____

_____

_____

_____

_____

_____

_____

_____

_____

_____

_____

_____

_____

_____

Your daughter,

Mi Cara—I love you!

Abba Father, Daddy God!

ABOUT THE AUTHOR

"But God has chosen the foolish things of the world to put to shame the wise, and God has chosen the weak things of the world to put to shame the things which are mighty; and the base things of the world and the things which are despised God has chosen, and the things which are not, to bring to nothing the things that are, that no flesh should glory in His presence."

1 Corinthians 1:27–29

I have the words "that's me!" written next to the above text in my bible. There's no false humility here, trust me. It's ironic of God to use me to write Letters from Heaven, a book about the Father heart of God. Me — a naturally fatherless child!

I was born and raised in the small island of Trinidad and Tobago until age 14, when I joined my mother in Connecticut. What a culture shock — I'm still recovering from winter!

My journey since then has led me to live in several states, including California, Texas and during the writing of this book, Kansas City, Missouri.

I have no theological, seminary education, training or credentials, but plenty real-time, hands-on experience with life.

I enjoy writing, reading, gardening and spending time with my precious granddaughters, Myah, Makayla and Emma.

Enough said. My prayer is that this writing has encouraged and blessed you to fall more in love with our Lord and to lean on Him, and Him only, through every experience, and that you bless others as you are blessed.

You've heard some of my story. I would love to hear yours!

You can reach me at: wave.transitions@gmail.com

Bible References

The majority of the Bible References came from the NKJV, ESV and/or the NIV.

My favorite Authors and Books

A few of my favorite authors and books include (in no particular order):

- Dietrich Bonhoeffer, "The Cost of Discipleship"
- Hannah Hurnard's "Hinds Feet on High Places"
- A.W. Tozer, "The Knowledge of the Holy"
- Andrew Murray, "Humility"
- Oswald Chambers "My Utmost for His Highest" Daily Devotional
- Beth Moore
- Kay Arthur
- Dr. Tony Evans
- Dr. Jack Hayford
- Henry T. Blackaby & Claude V. King
- Dr. Charles Stanley

Thank You. I join you in looking forward to the day when we awaken in His likeness. Blessings.

The LORD will accomplish
what concerns me;
Your loving kindness,
O LORD,
is everlasting;
Do not forsake
the work of your hands.
Psalm 138:8

Letters from heaven, for such a time as this......

CPSIA information can be obtained
at www.ICGtesting.com
Printed in the USA
FFOW05n1856151215